Radiant Hearts

Radiant Hearts

Bahá'í Prayers and Passages for Children

BELLWOOD
PRESS®

EVANSTON, ILLINOIS

Bellwood Press
1233 Central St., Evanston, IL 60202

Printed in the United States of America
on acid-free paper ∞

ISBN: 978-1-61851-242-0
28 27 26 25   4 3 2

Book and cover design by Patrick Falso
Illustrations by Aleisha Atashband

Prayers

Blessed is the spot, and the house, and the place, and the city, and the heart, and the mountain, and the refuge, and the cave, and the valley, and the land, and the sea, and the island, and the meadow where mention of God hath been made, and His praise glorified.

~ Bahá'u'lláh

Thy name is my healing, O my God, and remembrance of Thee is my remedy. Nearness to Thee is my hope, and love for Thee is my companion. Thy mercy to me is my healing and my succor in both this world and the world to come. Thou, verily, art the All-Bountiful, the All-Knowing, the All-Wise.

~ *Bahá'u'lláh*

He is God! O God, my God! Bestow upon me a pure heart, like unto a pearl.

~ *'Abdu'l-Bahá*

O God, guide me, protect me, make of me a shining lamp and a brilliant star. Thou art the Mighty and the Powerful.

~ *'Abdu'l-Bahá*

O Thou Kind Lord! I am a little child, exalt me by admitting me to the kingdom. I am earthly, make me heavenly; I am of the world below, let me belong to the realm above; gloomy, suffer me to become radiant; material, make me spiritual, and grant that I may manifest Thine infinite bounties.

Thou art the Powerful, the All-Loving.

~ 'Abdu'l-Bahá

O Lord! Plant this tender seedling in the garden of Thy manifold bounties, water it from the fountains of Thy loving-kindness and grant that it may grow into a goodly plant through the outpourings of Thy favor and grace.

Thou art the Mighty and the Powerful.

~ 'Abdu'l-Bahá

Passages from the Bahá'í Writings

O Son of Spirit! My first counsel is this: Possess a pure, kindly and radiant heart ...

~ *Bahá'u'lláh*

Tread ye the path of justice, for this, verily, is the straight path.

~ *Bahá'u'lláh*

O Friend! In the garden of thy heart plant naught but the rose of love . . .

~ Bahá'u'lláh

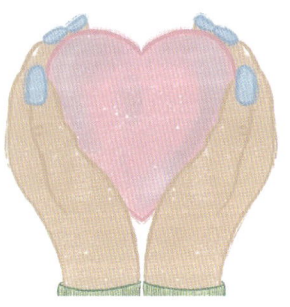

To give and to be generous are attributes of Mine; well is it with him that adorneth himself with My virtues.

~ *Bahá'u'lláh*

Blessed is he who preferreth his brother before himself.

~ Bahá'u'lláh

O Son of Man! Rejoice in the gladness of thine heart, that thou mayest be worthy to meet Me and mirror forth My beauty.

~ *Bahá'u'lláh*

O Son of Man! Humble thyself before Me, that I may graciously visit thee.

~ *Bahá'u'lláh*

Let your adorning be forgiveness and mercy and that which cheereth the hearts of the well-favored of God.

~ Bahá'u'lláh

Beautify your tongues, O people, with truthfulness, and adorn your souls with the ornament of honesty.

~ *Bahá'u'lláh*

Know that thy true adornment consisteth in the love of God and in thy detachment from all save Him . . .

~ Bahá'u'lláh

The source of all glory is acceptance of whatsoever the Lord hath bestowed, and contentment with that which God hath ordained.

~ Bahá'u'lláh

Blessed is he who mingleth with all men in a spirit of utmost kindliness and love.

~ Bahá'u'lláh

The source of courage and power is the promotion of the Word of God and steadfastness in His Love.

~ Bahá'u'lláh

Trustworthiness is the greatest portal leading unto the tranquility and security of the people.

~ *Bahá'u'lláh*

Be ye enkindled, O people, with the heat of the love of God, that ye may enkindle the hearts of others.

~ *Bahá'u'lláh*

O Son of Being! Thou art My lamp and My light is in thee. Get thou from it thy radiance and seek none other than Me.

~ Bahá'u'lláh

Happy is the faithful one who is attired with the vesture of high endeavor and hath arisen to serve this Cause.

~ *Bahá'u'lláh*

He, verily, shall increase the reward of them that endure with patience.

~ *Bahá'u'lláh*

Supremely lofty will be thy station, if thou remainest steadfast in the Cause of thy Lord.

~ Bahá'u'lláh

Truthfulness is the foundation
of all human virtues.

~ *'Abdu'l-Bahá*

We should at all times manifest our truthfulness and sincerity . . .

~ *'Abdu'l-Bahá*

Be thou happy. Be thou grateful. Arise to render thanks unto God, that thy thankfulness may conduce to an increase of bounty.

~ *'Abdu'l-Bahá*

The kingdom of God is founded upon equity and justice, and also upon mercy, compassion, and kindness to every living soul.

~ *'Abdu'l-Bahá*

Never lose thy trust in God. Be thou ever hopeful, for the bounties of God never cease to flow upon man.

~ 'Abdu'l-Bahá